Bad luck, Sam

T0372073

One morning, Sam tips
the milk carton but there
is no milk left.

Then he drops his mug and
spills his drink on the mat.

He bends down to pick up the mug and his shorts split!

Having a bit of bad luck, Sam?

Next, he brushes his hair
and the brush snaps!

Sam puts on his jacket
and the zip gets stuck.

He moans, "What a bad
luck morning for me!"

Sam trots to the bus stop to meet his pal, Asher.

Asher is there, but
the bus has just left.

Asher tells Sam, "No stress. Let's just go and shoot some hoops."

Sam lifts his foot and sees
that he is stuck to some gum!

Sam and Asher jog to the
park. Sam trips on a stick
and lands in a full bin.

Asher pulls him up.

That was a bit of bad luck for you.

At the park, Asher shoots
at the hoop and gets it in.

Sam aims and shoots but
misses. He keeps missing.

In the end, Sam says to Asher, "I quit! Let's just go. I am having no luck here at all."

Words to blend

morning	carton	park
down	hair	moans
Asher	meet	keeps
shoot	hoops	foot
aims	milk	stress
drops	shorts	spills
stuck	left	bends

Before reading

Synopsis: Sam is not having a good day. He is having bad luck. His friend Asher tries to cheer him up.

Review graphemes/phonemes: or ar ow air oa er ee oo ai

Story discussion: Look at the cover and read the title together. Ask: *How do you think Sam feels in the picture? What do you think will happen to Sam in this story?*

Link to prior learning: Display a word with adjacent consonants from the story, e.g. *brushes*. Ask children to put a dot under each single-letter grapheme (b, r, u, e, s) and a line under the digraph (*sh*). Model, if necessary, how to sound out and blend the adjacent consonants together to read the word. Repeat with another word from the story, e.g. *stick*, and encourage the children to sound out and blend the word independently.

Vocabulary check: shoot hoops – score points in basketball

Decoding practice: Ask children to turn to page 3. How quickly can they find and read the word *drink*? Can they find another word with adjacent consonants on this page? (*drops, spills*)

Tricky word practice: Display the word *one* and explain that all of this word is tricky! The *o* makes a /wu/ sound, and the *ne* makes a /n/ sound. Practise writing and reading this word.

After reading

Apply learning: Ask: *Can you remember some of the reasons Sam was having such a bad morning?* Check that children can remember at least some of the reasons; encourage them to look back at the story if necessary.

Comprehension

- What was the first thing that went wrong for Sam?
- Where did Sam and Asher go when they missed the bus?
- Do you think Sam feels better at the end of the story? Why or why not?

Fluency

- Pick a page that most of the group read quite easily. Ask them to reread it with pace and expression. Model how to do this if necessary.
- Encourage children to read Asher's words on page 10, making their reading sound natural and fluent.
- Practise reading the words on page 17.

Tricky words review

one	there	no
here	of	he
me	go	you
pulls	says	all
puts	what	full